Bestiary

Also by Donika Kelly

The Renunciations

Bestiary

Poems

Donika Kelly

Winner of the Cave Canem Poetry Prize
Selected by Nikky Finney

◙ ◙ ◙

Graywolf Press

This publication is made possible, in part, by the voters of Minnesota through
a Minnesota State Arts Board Operating Support grant, thanks to a legislative
appropriation from the arts and cultural heritage fund, and through a grant
from the Wells Fargo Foundation Minnesota. Significant support has also
been provided by Target, the McKnight Foundation, the Amazon Literary
Partnership, and other generous contributions from foundations, corpora-
tions, and individuals. To these organizations and individuals we offer our
heartfelt thanks.

Published by Graywolf Press
212 Third Avenue North, Suite 485
Minneapolis, Minnesota 55401

www.graywolfpress.org

Published in the United States of America

ISBN 978-1-55597-758-0

8   10   12   14   15   13   11   9

Library of Congress Control Number: 2016931145

Cover design: Jeenee Lee Design

Cover art: Artist unknown. *Adam Naming the Animals,* c. 1250–1260, England.
Digital image courtesy of the Getty's Open Content Program.

For Beth, Christardra, Drema, Valri, and Vida

Contents

Introduction

A first book is a migration story. It is a leave-taking from the old rules and rulers. Turn. Rotate. In this migration story, a poet returns west in order finally to set sail. There is death in the home-going. There is sweet birth. Opening the wide door wide will require a hammer of words.

The poet learns what trust is and isn't. What real is and what real isn't. A liquor store and a beauty shop are on fire behind her. The poet can smell the pomade and the alcohol burning together. She whistles and crows as she gathers up everything she can. We follow her because the suitcase she is holding is smoldering with all of us in it. She stands there holding on tight to the grip's hot handle. We read and blow on our own fire-eaten hands as we turn. Keep turning. The screen of pages, as you will see, keeps changing from little girl on fire to burning ancient Los Angeles, to sex. She will not look away anymore. The poet who is writing of the narrator's undoing has refused to be undone and disappears somewhere into the ink without warning. Turn.

I found this first book of Donika Kelly's poems to be made of red bricks and seashells, poem material so old you can still smell the salt in them—from before—when the city the poet is returning to was not a city at all. Some of the poems sit squat in the middle of the page like something you could throw and break a window with. Some of the poems fall down the page like the ladder required to climb inside that broken window. There is always the glimmer and glint of hope in these poems peering out, even as the page smolders. On the map itself, there are places where blood has been spilled. There are places where screams went ignored. Rotate. Turn. See the daughter finally stop running from herself.

Keep reading and you realize this poet rests her alphabets in the mythology of fire and the resurrection of ecstasy. She is gripped in a blaze that has never gone out, that has continued to burn underground, in the safety of a daughter's only, orange-light horizon. See the mother. See the resurrection. Move on.

The poet has decided to run into the many rooms of memory. She has clearly drawn her weapons. She knows trees: fig, walnut, and olive. She knows birds: blue bower, cave swallow, hermit thrush. She knows Greek mythology. A minotaur can sometimes be seen running outside the window. The minotaur keeps up with her Black girl life.

Bestiary is a first book of poems by an all Black girl who teaches us nothing is all black, or all female, or all male, or all belonging to humans, or all tidy. Bestiaries come out of an old tradition, but the beasts that push us to write our modern migration stories are found everywhere we dare deeply look. A hybrid of longing and lust is chronicled and mapped out here. What has been made contains a compass of new measuring. An inch is now a foot swinging at the father's head.

Before it is over and the last page turned, we will discover that the poet is not afraid to close her eyes around every winged thing she can find. We will see she has great need of elevators and anything else that will lift her from the ashes. Levitation. Rotation. Landing. She walks strongly and confidently, right up to the live thing, and then pushes her tongue deep into the skin of a patch of black walnut trees in order to hear what she really needs to hear. She is measuring out what she needs in order to leap.

Kelly's first poetic report to the world would not be complete without including the national-pastime party drinks of Black people: pink panties, screwdrivers, and that smoothest of smooth operator, Canadian Club. Reverence is held onto for that most sacred Black card game, Spades, the one that is tattooed on the back of every Black person's hand born before circa 1980. Rotate. Turn.

The official public record tells us there are hundreds of years of unreliable others imagining and appropriating the desires of Black girls, eschewing their hopes and dreams as poets and people, their birth-marked stories, their personal migrations. For the other record, let me say, those reports have never had anything to do with Black girls and whales, Black girls and riots, Black girls and minotaurs, centaurs, satyrs, mermaids, werewolves, or Black girls "being a thing that breaks before it bends." Black girls have always and often been the whispered-about and the strangely labeled. Not enough Black girls, whose own personal stories could turn you to stone with just a whisper, their up-the-side-of-the-mountain migrations rarely published or *allowed* to be told. But here is one that I have pulled from the great pile into the light so we might add it to the small truth pile of others. In *Bestiary,* no bending will be allowed. Rotate.

Kelly catalogs the scribbling girl heart switching and swooning, sweating, remembering, chiseling—memories cradled upright into the unholy light of childhood's LED lights. A migration of pure trust. The poet finds the cadence and courage to morph into wired-hair, mythical Griffon, the pointing dog known for its even temperament, rough coat, and bearded muzzle. Turn to midnight, turn to the father who is also there at midnight, "walking from his room to mine," after which the poet begins whistling—and crowing too. Rotate. Turn. Remember the old churchwomen who twisted our ears and warned us about "the whistling woman and the crowing hen?" How righteously they dangled that stand-alone brazen woman before our eyes, believing that if they did we might be scared enough to be "good girls" and stay in line. Remember how they warned us we would come to No Good if we followed the whistling crowing woman? Please follow closely.

Come inside. Kelly's first book is a compendium of rocks, ledges, whistles, and edges. These poems come complete with their ithy-phallic males, with their eye-to-eye looking at each other and their permanent erections. Kelly introduces a human obsidian cast of characters, alongside the poet's bright-speckled granite memory, spilling with nests made of translucent stones, blood, and floating feathers from the long, preening migration journey of girl to wom-an. Harder things are held high. There are also the brutal, bruising, unexpected drops straight down.

In order to find comfort or truth, or both, we are not allowed to leave the poet's journey too soon, not before the narrator takes the time to see herself as a serious student of male porn, "Only the boys for me now, hard / bellied and fucking." A narrator who loved cartwheels and was always afraid of riots and the Pacific air on fire finally makes it to the land of her birth, turning her own intimate pandemonium into olive trees, turning the fires on the edge of town into the mating call of the whistling female thrush. Looking it all right in the eye.

Donika Kelly whistles and crows her book into a psalm of pure re-solve. And in the end, no mythology remains. Everything is singed and true. A report has been filed on the poet's behalf. A Black girl has whistled and warbled into the morning and night air and duti-fully weighed in with her long black pen. A new song has been measured out from the ancient rubble of Los Angeles and the poet's own four-chambered muscle. *Bestiary*'s lesson is complicated and also simple. Love can be hunted down.

Nikky Finney

Bestiary

Out West

Refuse the old means of measurement.
Rely instead on the thrumming
wilderness of self. Listen.

You have been lost for some time,
taking comfort in being home
to any wandering thing. Sheep and brown cows

graze your heart pocket. Antelope and bison
lap the great lake of your eye. And in your ear
the black bear winters.

You name your dawn shadow
Rabbit.

You name your dusk shadow
Spur.

And the river that cuts you as it runs west,
you name it Persistence.

Look. If you could bear sobriety,
you'd be sober.

If you could bear
being a person, you would no longer be
an iron bluff.

Do not wander. We are all apportioned
a certain measure of stillness.

"Oh, monsters are scared . . .
That's why they're monsters."

—NEIL GAIMAN

Catalogue

You think about being small,
a child. No. Smaller,
a bird. Smaller still,
a small bird. You think
about the art of holding,
of being held. This hand
can crush you.
Pulp and feather you.
Could release the air
from all your little bones.

You grow. You are large.
You are a 19th century poem.
All of America is inside you,
a catalogue of lives and land
and burrowing things. You contain
your beloved: a field, a building
of softening wood. The birds.
Always. The birds.

Soon you will be a person. Nothing
will change. Your body will be of a piece
with all other bodies: the thrush,
the dormouse, the great black bear.
When you open your mouth,
there will be only air.
Tighten your throat. Sound,
inexplicably, like something lost.

Fourth Grade Autobiography

We live in Los Angeles, California.
We have a front yard and a backyard.
My favorite things are cartwheels, salted plums,
and playing catch with my dad. I squeeze the grass
and dirt between my fingers. Eat my tongue
white. He launches every ball into orbit.
Every ball drops like an anvil, heavy
and straight into my hands. I am afraid
of riots and falling and the dark.
The sunset of flames ringing our block,
groceries and Asian-owned storefronts. No one
to catch me. Midnight walks from his room to mine.
I believe in the devil.
I have a sister and a brother
and a strong headlock. We have a dog named
Spunky, fawn and black. We have an olive
tree. A black walnut tree. A fig tree.
We lie in the grass and wonder who writes
in the sky. I lie in the grass and imagine
my name, a cloud drifting. Saturday
dance parties. Everyone drunk on pink
panties, screw drivers, and Canadian Club.
Dominoes and spades. Al Green and Mack 10.
Sometimes Mama dances with the dog.
Sometimes my dad dances with me. I am
careful not to touch. He is careful
to smile with his whole face.

Where she is opened. Where she is closed.

When he opens her chest, separates the flat skin
of one breast from the other, breaks the hinge of ribs,
and begins, slowly, to evacuate her organs, she is silent.

He hollows her like a gourd, places her heart
below her lungs, scrapes the ribs clean of fat
and gristle with his thick fingers. He says, *Now you are ready,*

and climbs inside. But she is not ready for the dry bulk
of his body curled inside her own. She is not ready to exhale
his breath, cannot bear both him and herself,

but he says, *Carry me,* and she carries him beneath her
knitted ribs, her hard breasts. He is the heart now,
the lungs and stomach that she cannot live without.

Love Poem: Chimera

I thought myself lion and serpent. Thought
myself body enough for two, for we.
Found comfort in never being lonely.

What burst from my back, from my bones, what lived
along the ridge from crown to crown, from mane
to forked tongue beneath the skin. What clamor

we made in the birthing. What hiss and rumble
at the splitting, at the horns and beard,
at the glottal bleat. What bridges our back.

What strong neck, what bright eye. What menagerie
are we. What we've made of ourselves.

Bower

Consider the bowerbird and his obsession
of blue, and then the island light, the acacia,
the grounded beasts. Here, the iron smell of blood,
the sweet marrow, fields of grass and bone.

And there, the bowerbird.
Watch as he manicures his lawn, puts in all places
a bit of blue, a turning leaf. And then,
how the female finds him,
lacking. All that blue for nothing.

Hermit Thrush

We never knew winter before this.
Winter where none of the trees lose

their needles,
where ice creaks the limb,

and the hermit thrush forages for insects
on the forest floor. Winter where,

finally, the white girls, after a long,
long summer of bronze and muscle and shine,

cover their legs. Winter, where we can finally feel
beautiful, too.

We say we.
I mean I.

When they cover their legs,
I can feel beautiful, too.

Bower

The bowerbird finds
a bluer eye to line his nest,
his groomed ground,
his wooing place.

The bluer eye does break
and weep when the bowerbird
leaves or brings
leaves or branches or bits
of simple blue string.

The bluer eye does look and look
and flinch at the open beak,
the narrow maw,
the trauma of being dug
deeper into the arched
and closing bower.

The bowerbird had lost
his sense of blue, his sense
of eye, but the string tangles,
beautifully, on his dark, clean grounds.

Self-Portrait as a Block of Ice

What the tongue wants.
Supplication and the burn
of crystals expanding.

To be, always, a waxing,
a waning, and, in waxing
again, not ever the same.

Waste and deferral.
Accumulation and deferral.
You are flesh,

and you are water,
though of the flesh,
you are only muscle,

and of the water,
you are saltless and clean.
Be a caution, a reckoning,

be a thing that breaks
before it bends.

Bower

A small hat, the fedora,
gray-blue banded tweed,
sits atop an unkempt nest,

my unpicked hair, a bromeliad
in the canopy. This
is a failure,

this ill-fitted hat. These boy things.
These men things. This hurried
disrobing. My ashen body

and untrimmed nails. But who will listen
to the song of a nutbrown hen?

Self-Portrait as a Door

All the birds die of blunt-force trauma—
of barn of wire of YIELD or SLOW
CHILDREN AT PLAY. You are a sign
are a plank are a raft are a felled oak.
You are a handle are a turn are a bit
of brass lovingly polished.
What birds what bugs what soft
hand come knocking. What echo
what empty what room in need
of a picture a mirror a bit of paint
on the wall. There is a hooked rug.
There is a hand hard as you are hard
pounding the door. There is the doormat
owl eye patched by a boot by a body
with a tree for a hand. What roosts
what burrows what scrambles
at the pound. There is a you
on the other side, cold and white
as the room, in need of a window
or an eye. There is your hand
on the door which is now the door
pretending to be a thing that opens.

Swallow

The first time you swallow—
the light, lurid and cold—

you know you mean
to swallow—again and again—

a woman's voice crawling and heavy
in your body, trying to escape.

Stay calm. You cannot let go.
There isn't an abstraction
you believe in and you are sad for it.

You need a mission to return to,
you need a flock to follow.

Love Poem: Pegasus

Foaled, fully grown, from my mother's neck,
her severed head, the silenced snakes. Call this

freedom. My first cry, a beating of wings,
abandon. Call me orphan before I
even know what a mother is. I think

myself a rising, feather and hoof, neigh
and caw, and you, always, on my back.

You bear a sword and shield, remind me
of her labor, her stoning gaze. What beast

will your blade free next? What call will you loose
from another woman's throat?

Handsome is

In the dream, my father hides inside
another man's body.
                              I know him
by his hands. But how am I child?
And this wall against my back, how long
has it been a wall? My father follows
me. Handsome as a close friend,
a tree in bloom.
I build a room to hold him.
He picks all the locks. I scream.
                              Don't scream.
I run. Stand still. I am a forest,
a field. I crumble and shift. I wake,
my breath deep inside the earth.

How to be alone

Not that you ever are. The small, rough
dogs lie at your feet or warm your belly.
Who make bearable all that you must
bear. What needs doing, regularly. You
fear your life without them; the hawk
perched on your roof, eyeing the
smaller. The larger, safe for now.

Practice the lonely drag that makes you
no different from the men you resemble.
Let this be a kind of safety. The
shamble in your walk. Become
invulnerable in holding, on every body,
your eye, roving, restless.

This heartache like any cliché, sincere
and boring. The small dogs your only
constant. You call the smallest to your
breast. The larger, belly exposed,
snoring. They rest.

Admit that, were you a different kind
of person, you would smash in your
father's skull with your booted foot.
This being a fantasy you can hear and
smell and all but feel. A father one
hates. No mother to speak of.

Admit also your mother's death.
Mention, often, her resurrection; the
load of the word. Remember how she
grieved, freshly, when she asked if her
mother was truly dead. How you
answered yes. How she forgot. How
you killed her mother, again and again.

Because she leaves.
And you are always your best.
And you are a fool.
Because you believe in reciprocity.
Because you are afraid of your own
hand. How could you have asked her to
stay?

The couch being, at this juncture and many others, the best antidote to loneliness. Narrow and brown. You know the small dogs will wake you when the neighbor leaves for work, crow and shrill. You know you will yell at the littlest and larger to return to the fetal S of your body.

Crumple the fetal S of your body until
you resemble a ball of paper. The fold
of your limbs, the ache in your joints.
You are too young to be so sore. You
make no room for the rough dogs now.
Your boys. It is winter. You are miserly
with heat.

You plan to get the larger one fixed.
You joke, *there are no balls in my
house,* but this is not a joke. Your
father, whose head you would make a
mess of, is oddly attached to the larger's
balls. You consider how the neutering
will affect him. The father. Weeping
over the end of his name.

The smaller has crawled between you
and your green hoodie. Your house is
cold. You have been cruel to the woman
you love because she has been honest
with you. You embarrass yourself.
What you crave: distance. What the
smaller gives you: warmth.

Home is where your dogs are. Home is
where your gods are. Your feet are quite
cold. Still the smallest trembles on your
belly. *You* continues to become *her.*
The misfiring keyboard. Operator. I
might be dying. Dead. Soon, like my
mother, who finally remembered my
name.

Only the boys. The couch is best
tonight, though the wind pries sound
from all the loose parts of this house
and so pries the gruff and gutter of my
sweetest hearts. I would like to sleep.
That I might bear what needs it.

Admit also cutting. The attempted
suicides. Both. And the little
ways you brick up your heart. Admit
the sweet black of charcoal making a
river of your body. The blackest you've
ever been.

The louvered windows. The peach
walls. The buckling ceiling that needs
repair. The gusset of your panties
soaked with your father's semen. Why
you no longer wear panties. Why he
deserves every arc of your boot. Why
the door is always locked.

She, a zombie. Undead. Specter of
herself. Mother. Mama. She does not
remember to think of me anymore. We
recognize each other only in echoes.

Your sadness is full of sadness. You
feel as a man feels: reluctantly. Your
feet are still cold. Oh, little and larger
ones who keep you warm. Oh, little and
larger ones who guard the little lock of
your peace.

Whale

Know, first, that she does not remain
behind the baleen forever.

Know, too, that the whale is unaware
of the woman drowning on its tongue.

And knowing this, recall the keening,
the slow build of sound in the body;

that we were afraid and pressed our fear
low in our breast, held it alongside our breath;

that the tenor of our grief matched,
so nearly, the tenor of our hysteria;

how finally there was no whale
or breath or sound or woman;

how, finally, there was only the body,
rising through the water toward the sun.

Ceremony at the end of a season

The season
was winter.

The sky filled the branches
with water.

The wind filled the branches
with ice.

The sun filled the branches
with light.

The tree was dying.

The branches snapped
like fingers.

I gnarled and gnashed
the tree.

I crushed my tongue
into the knotted bark.

I filled the buckets
with salt

from my own
body.

I buried them
beneath the tree.

Ostrich

for RR

The birds are spare here:
more air
than marrow in their small bones.

There is a we,
also spare, more fracture
than sense. This we, on the red
metal swing, figure one

another with desire
and failure: to be knowable,
to be known.
But no.

No reciprocal dance
of recognition. No mirroring
eye, but brooding,
                    brooding. And the mosquitoes
and the drooping birds,
and the waiting for a deepening night.

Arkansas Love Song

Fences break a landscape
the way a body makes
a road—somewhere between

Memphis and home,
the shoulder collects masses
of hide and blood and white,

white tendon. The road binds
us, one to another,
and I try to make the binding

mean something about
forgetting and the failures
of resurrection. This

is a failure. The disarticulated
wing stands for a disarticulated
wing. The rusted breast, the same.

This is not about my mother.
Another failure.
It is about nothing else.

A man goes west and falls off his horse in the desert

The horse gallops into the sun with a ghost on his back.
The horse like a memory racing away.

He is smaller than the butte, is smaller than the desert,
is smaller than the sky.

A setting sun.
A broken leg.

The man feels his chest. Am I a ghost?
His lungs reply: *You are the bravest stone.*

O, how the sky stretches like skin above him!
He wonders that it doesn't split at his voice.

Love Poem: Centaur

Nothing approaches a field like me. Hard
gallop, hard chest—hooves and mane and flicking
tail. My love: I apprehend each flower,
each winged body, saturated in a light
that burnishes. I would make a burnishing
of you, by which I mean a field in flower,
by which I mean, a breaching—my hands
making an arrow of themselves, rooting
the loosened dirt. I would make for you
the barest of sounds, wing against wing,
there, at the point of articulation. Love,
I pound the earth for you. I pound the earth.

Secretary

Bend your leg
back. Bend your leg
like this secretary

bird. Stomp that lizard
dead. Long leg, bird
leg. You got small

lives to eat. You got
a dance to do: mate.
Them girls don't come
on their own. Spread

your wings like legs,
wide. Put some air
in your bones.

Love Poem: centaur

I have never known a field as wild
as your heart. Or galloped or hardened
my breast in the sun. I call my own bluff
and bravado: what I apprehend needs
no apprehension; what I make, stands
undone. Here is my hand, soft, uncalloused.
Here, a lock of my mane. Now, I am afraid
and so I turn to the field. The flower
and red beetle and winter light. The cardinal
hen. Your pretty brown bird cutting the sky.

Love Poem: Satyr

I have filed my horns and trimmed my beard
and warmed my throat into a fine and sober
warble. I play a little song in the key

of your name. I call to you with a breath
of spring, a small wind warmed in my breast
and shaped by the lips you loved. Love, I see

you've closed the window to your heart.
Closed, too, the door, and blacked the light.
I put my ear to the glass, to the wood. I hear

your heart like the wind in the reeds,
meting out my name.

Balloon

She thinks skin a little balloon
and blood a little ballast.
What kind of bird is she? Foul.
What kind of woman is she?
The groan skating her throat
sounds like a promise.
Something hurts.
Wants out.

Love Poem: Mermaid

Do you ever look into a mirror,
which is also an ocean heavy with sun?

Do you ever pull your hair,
wet, over your shoulder to dry

as you sit and sing for another's
death? Love, I am made

for calling: bare breast, smooth tail,
the perfect balance of scales.

I have claimed this rock,
which is also your heart,

which is also a shell I hold
to my ear to hear what is right

in front of me. I am a witness
to the sea and the sun, to your body

lashed to the mast. O that my voice
were a knife, that a knife could change

anything, that there was nothing
between us but salt and breath.

Love letter

I wake each morning.
And am disappointed in the waking.

In the evening, in the hours before sleep,
I drag canyons into my forearms, dredge

the little tributaries of mud and fish.
These pits and hollows make a mess of everything

they touch. I am reeling, spooling
away from what holds muscle to bone.

Tumbling from what holds me to the world.
O, to do away with the meat and light of me.

Love Poem: Werewolf

At the threshold, your hand heavies, widens
into a fist. A knock. The door's yellow

eye mocks you, and you wish your back would split.
You wish the coat would burst from your skin.

You have no patience. You are full of want
and marrow. The moon is new and new this

desire to be your heaviest self.
Again, you knock. Again, the mocking eye.

You damn the moon its darkness, your shuffling
boots, your impotent hands. You have a howl

for this dark well. It sifts out a whimper.

Little Box

The woman you love is afraid she is hurting you.
This is the source of her fear. You are afraid
to say, *I am hurting*. You are crying.

You are afraid your parents will discover
that you are crying, again, and send you, again, to therapy
where a woman with long hair and a long skirt

will point to the dollhouse and ask where the mother
doll sleeps. And the father. And, if they have a child,
where the child doll sleeps.

You speak in therapy. Every statement begins,
I feel—, even when you mean, *why are you hurting me?*
You'd rather be a simpler animal.

You try to imagine what the bear feels.
The seal. The otter. Always a little group of three.
You worry they are not, in fact, simpler, but you are sure

they are never lonely. You hate your loneliness
as you hated yourself as a child. You are bored
with your hatred. You want her to stop hurting you.

You want to say, *I love you*, again and again.
This will change nothing. And, you've already said it.
When you were a child in therapy, you understood

where each doll went. You learned not to cry.
There is no teacher now to tell your parents,
and anyway, your mother doesn't remember you,

and you are settling into hating your father,
though, you are afraid you are as careless and cruel
as they taught you to be. You will see your therapist

in two weeks. Her hair is short and she is from the same city
as the woman you love. You will tell her you are sad
and hurting. You will be matter of fact. You will think

of the seal, a mother perhaps, how she might be lonely
for a lost pup. But there will be another, and she will forget
the one that was eaten by an orca or polar bear or neglect.

You will tell your therapist none of this.
You will no longer speak to the woman who has your heart.
You will put her in the room farthest away from your own.
She will sleep where the father should be.

Self-Portrait as a Wooden Flower

Small wound.
Bark pulled from pale,
from white, from little twig.

Dark bark, and inside
a light that gathers and curls
before the knife.

Commandments

Abstain from the field,
from the hollow boned earth, the thick
bones of winter.

Abstention means abandon.
Means sorrow.
Means remember.

Forgetting means the red wings smother
the grass, means the shell of an ear on a mountain
of bark.

Love is a religion.
Flesh is a religion.
Use the body like a drum.

And so, where once the field,
now a cave; where once the bird,
now a sky that belongs to the sea.

Fallow means all the fields are closed.
Closed means the earth is in the body,
means the body is full of wings.

Wings mean you are alive
and someone is not. Alive means
you swallow each day like a stone.

Love Poem: Griffon

I am busy.
Busy guard
dog. Lion. What
kind of bird am I?
Lazy, to sit here
so long, in the act
of guarding.
Call me priceless,
call me worthless,
mishmash, I am.
Hybrid, I am. Here,
let me hold you
in my paw.
Talon. Little mouse,
little chimney
sweep, little dream
I dreamed as I waited
for you to call me
lonely, on the building's
edge. Call the waiting
not what it is,
foolish, but
a kind of bravery,
a kind of patience.
Kindness. Here,
I have for you
a mouse, a boy
booted black,
an old dream.
See how he sits
in my paw.

Talon. Let me unfurl
that you might see
what fear looks like
in a small face.

Archaeology

More and more   I find the image of my father
in my own face   an emptiness behind the eyes
I am unable to move   the ore in my blood
slurried and slow   the sun bruising the sky
in its slow drag   I am dragging his face
out of my own   I am the sun and the sky
and the hot bruise   I squint against
my own light   which is my father's light
which is me   I am an archaeologist
sifting the grit of my muddled blood
There is nothing behind my eyes
but the stone   you left me
with him   you left
when he settled   into my face
a hot bruise   I am dragging
the sun   in my empty blood
more and more   I find in the image of ore
your muddled eyes   you are unable to move
Archaeologist   you sift my face
which is his   which is stone.

Tender

My sister says *tender* into the phone
like a woman who believes only in the idea
of woman. She says *young tender,*

and it is the 1990s and our parents still love
one another and they slow drag in the living
room and we are too young to do anything but ride

our bikes and wrestle in the grass and dream
about being grown, the wonder of another body
pressed to our own. Our father

has the biggest arms and the softest hair in the world.
Our mother remembers everything.
Young tender, and the sky is full

of words; we have only just discovered
how clouds move, what crooning
means, whip appeal, and something is breaking

ground in our bodies. *Legal tender.*
I am laughing into the phone in a voice that sounds
like crying. I am crying at my sister's drawl,

drawing *tender* through two decades and halfway
across the country. My sister a mother now,
holding on to tenderness, though she is afraid

of what her body can no longer do. My father
slow dragging in another town. My mother content
with the idea of memory, with what has been lost.

Winter Poem

We climb the stalk of early winter
into the sky. Below: the car, the road,
the gray branch. The sun, a mirage, multiplies
in the earth. The light beetles, makes of our
bodies a mirror. We are fallow
as the land beneath us. We climb, though our
arms tire and our legs burn, a gesture
of absolution—we forget,
are forgotten. We are fire or
the image of fire, the day, or
the breaking of it. We disappear, chaff
of myth, what held the story of a season's end.

Love Poem: Donika

This is a spring of shambles.
Of meadows slow to flower,
of fire sooting the underbrush,
and, love, I am lonely as a bear.

I am no good at bearish things.
Fish or forage, my hands
are too small and slow to clip
the salmon thick in the heat
of spawn.
         I do not know where
berries are or honey or campers
or the greening branch.
I am tired of mounting
this hill alone.
         Love, how do I gain
what was lost in winter?

Red Bird

I learn to sleep with the doors open.
My legs open. The air full of water.

Locusts molt in perfect derivation,
green from brown. The red bird inside my chest,

between my knees. This red bird calls
like it is spring, like a brown hen will cock

her head and answer. We are in the full
throat of summer, my red bird and I.

The locust, whirring in the redbud;
unhusking itself on brick, too large now

for its old, parchment body.
I rub my legs together.

I let water out of the air.
I am full throated and calling.

What Gay Porn Has Done for Me

Only the boys for me now, hard
bellied and fucking.

Or fucked.

Call it comfort, or truth, how they look,
not at the camera, as women do,
but at one another.

Or to god.

How they know where their faces go.
They open their mouths. They spread
their cheeks. They come on everything.

On everything.

Each body is a body on display,
and one I am meant to see and desire.

I am learning to love
the look of men. I am learning

what to do with my face,
and I come on anything I like.

Sonnet in which only one bird appears

When did one season begin and another end?
What branched like a nerve? What burrowed
like a heart? Can we say *love?*
What will the yellowing tree bear?

◧

Between each rib, cartilage and blood.
Beneath this cage of bone, four chambers.
Inside each chamber, you, throbbing,
compelling the blood and air.

◧

There is a body I hold like a sound,
a name my mind cradles like a pit
on the tongue. But where is the flesh?
And how will it weigh my palm?

◧

If we can say *love,* here is the ocean.
Here the white bird of your heart.
Here the hard sun and sand. Here a town

closed for the season, a man wearing
all his clothes, asleep on the beach.
We say mountain. We say nothing.

We make a cross on the sand. We discover
the wonder of perpendicularity.

Love Poem: Minotaur

Freedom is a thread of light snaking
the canyon like an ant through a conch.

A good-bye to each dead end and small room.
Salt, once of the sea, now of the wind,
now on my brow, making a witness of me.

I open my mouth to the wind. The wind
opens my heart, my breast. I leave the bare

bones behind. I leave the soul, once another's,
once my own, there in that maze of sand,

mortar, and bellows. A golden light hails
me, pulls me like a worm from the earth.

Santa Rosa

The red rock rises, a muscle
meant to replace what is no longer found
in air. Each butte and bitter lake

marks us, and there are men here.
I am afraid, but they are only fishing,
their poles divining water from sky.

We boulder over the lake,
far from home, and I cannot
lose you, though I shake like a wet cur.

I've forgotten which way is west,
how we ended up in this cooling desert.
I've forgotten, nearly, what I'm meant

to grieve. I am lost.
Walk with me, love,
that I might know what is real.

Love Poem

1   Come morning we are fish.
We flop and gasp and rub our scales
against one another. We iridesce
orange and green and shred the flannel
with our thrashing.

2   All day, away from you, I pine,
bark and needle. I break into the bank
of sky. Inside, there is a thick
ring, the newest ring. A season
of growth—of sun and water—

3   All day, away from me, I imagine you,
the sun and water. You are salt and space
and long, long arms of heat. Both the light
and what reflects it.

4   When I see you again, I am the strongest
man in the world. I hurl tires and pull trucks
with my breast for you.
You are also the strongest man
in the world. You carry barrels of cement
all over the house. When we arm wrestle,
I tell you, between gritted teeth, of my life as a tree:
How tall I was.
How brown and green.

5   At night, the bed is covered with pollen
and scales. The room is bright and wet.
My muscles are so small now.
I fill my lungs with the entirety
of your name, and your head
on my breast rises and sets. Rises and sets.

Back East

On the northern route we learn the difference
between the sloped and branching horns
of moose, elk, deer, antelope.

We drive north, then south, but always east.
We sing *I'm a tumbling tumbleweed,*
as we tumble south across the broad middle plains.

This road is a winding one.
We left the west flooded
with new loneliness.

We see buffalo on the yellow hill, quail in the brush.
We sing *a tumbling* to statues of elk
and snowy mountains always to our right.

Under a clear sky, your hand in mine. A hand full of sky . . .
Not song but description.
And this wind is a drying one.

Acknowledgments

Many thanks to the editors of the following venues in which versions of these poems appeared:

Bloom, "What Gay Porn Has Done for Me" and "Tender"
Crazyhorse, "Archaeology"
The Feminist Wire, "Whale," "Arkansas Love Song," and "Where she is opened. Where she is closed."
Gris-Gris, "Handsome is," "Little Box," and "Love letter"
Gulf Coast, "Love Poem: Chimera"
Hayden's Ferry Review, "Whale"
Indiana Review, "Arkansas Love Song"
Nashville Review, "Fourth Grade Autobiography"
Pleiades, "Love Poem: Centaur" and "Love Poem: Mermaid"
Quarterly West, "Ostrich"
TORCH, "Hermit Thrush" and "Secretary"
Tupelo Quarterly, "Self-Portrait as a Door" and "A man goes west and falls off his horse in the desert"
Vinyl, "Love Poem: Minotaur" and "Sonnet in which only one bird appears"
The Virginia Quarterly Review, "Bower (Consider the bowerbird)," "Swallow," and "How to be alone (Not that you ever are)"
West Branch, "Love Poem: Griffon"

This book would not have been possible without the kind and generous support of Vanderbilt University's English Department, Cave Canem, the Michener Center for Writers, the Department of English and Foreign Languages at Southern Arkansas University, and the Bucknell Seminar for Younger Poets.

All the feelings for all my people: Regina Ross, Samuel Penegar, Danita Ford, Makii, Mariah, Roland, and Major. Carlisha Bell, Ama Codjoe, Nikki Spigner, Matt Duques, Diana Bellonby, Monte Holman, Jessica Burch, Deborah Lilton, Destiny Birdsong, and Nafissa Thompson-Spires. Petal Samuels, Lucy Mensah, Stephanie Pruitt, Jill Schepmann, Katie Greene, Susanna Kwan, and Freya Sachs. Michael Kreyling, Dana Nelson, Teresa Goddu, Ifeoma Nwankwo, Mark Jarman, Rick Hilles, Nancy Reisman, Julie Fesmire, Rory Dicker, Ellen Armour, Barbee Majors, Janis May, Donna Caplan, and Margaret Quigley. Roger Reeves, Monica Jimenez, L. Lamar Wilson, Phillip B. Williams, Jericho Brown, and Nicole Sealey. Ansel Elkins and Leticia Trent. Miriam Greenburg, Domenica Ruta, Jim Magnuson, Marla Akin, A. Van Jordan, and Pat Rosal. Jenny Bell, Amber Baldwin, Sydney Minnerly, Shannon Dennis, and Jo Williams. Shannin and the Schroeder family, Linda Selman, and Elizabeth Davis.

Nikky Finney, thank you for seeing me.

Enormous thanks to Elizabeth Barnett for reading and rereading infinite drafts of this collection and for being my office wife.

Donika Kelly received an MFA in Writing from the Michener Center for Writers at the University of Texas at Austin, and a PhD in English from Vanderbilt University. She is a Cave Canem Fellow and was a June Fellow of the Bucknell Seminar for Younger Poets. Kelly's poems have appeared in *Indiana Review*, *Pleiades*, the *Virginia Quarterly Review*, and *West Branch*, among other publications. She teaches at the University of Iowa.

The text of *Bestiary* is set in Electra. Book design by Connie Kuhnz. Composition by Bookmobile Design and Publishing Services, Minneapolis, Minnesota. Manufactured by Versa Press on acid-free, 30 percent postconsumer wastepaper.